Patpong

Bangkok's twilight zone

A photographic diary

by

Nick Nostitz

"NOW YOU ANGRY ME,
YOU LOOK ME SAME DOG,
BUT AFTER YOU LOOK PUSSY ME,
YOU HAPPY TOO MUCH!"

introduction / Bangkok warriors

Patpong: two streets, a few side alleys, 1001 go-go bars, discos, blow-job bars, after hour joints, restaurants, pharmacies, VD clinics, bookstores, ████ offices, souvenir shops, a few massage parlours, one supermarket, one Kentucky Fried Chicken, one McDonalds. Nana Plaza: ██████ three floors of go-go bars, beer bars █ and a snooker hall. Soi Cowboy: an alley lined with go-go bars. A few gay clubs on Silom Soi 2 and 4. Washington Square, for Vietnam vets and middle-aged Americans. Buckskin Joe Village, beer bars under the expressway. Grace Hotel area█ : the Muslim world and Africans, occasional Russian hookers. Soi ████████ Taniya's hostess clubs for the Japanese (Japanese only). And, of course, the incredible Thermae.

Bangkok's twilight zone, sex'n'drugs'n'rock'n'roll. This is where the worlds meet, the rich, the poor, all cultures. In some rare moments of animalistic freedom, drunkenness and ecstasy, differences disappear, man, woman, man-woman.

A sexual underground where people get sucked in, changed, moulded, and eventually spat out.

Enjoy, but never love. Love makes you vulnerable. Love is the only thing that can't be bought here and, if found, is usually an illusion. Hedonism is pure - if rarely simple. You can leave the zone but it will never leave you.

WELCOME

ON ACID IN STAR OF LOVE,
8/2/94

ME + JONATHAN IN THERMAE
14/7/96

MY FIRST YEAR IN BANG-
KOK, A WINDOWLESS HOLE
DAYTIME SLEEPING, NIGHTS
OUT, WINTER '93

JEFF, IN LIPS II   6/10/93

George brought Jeff to Thailand. They met one day on the street in San Francisco, where George spent a few months after he got deported for the first time from Thailand for overstaying his ~~WORK~~ visa. George convinced Jeff to give him the money for an airline ticket, and off they went.

Jeff the philosopher only appeared every few weeks. Most of the time he was locked in his room, reading, writing, barely able to sleep, lost in the strange JOURNEYS ~~journeys~~ of his mind until the inevitable breakdown came. He tore up all his scribbled sheets and started drinking with George. Hitting Patpong, falling in love with the first hooker he saw. Explaining Nietzsche to her while she EMPTIED ~~emptied~~ his pockets, crying in some corner for a while, partying again. For days. One drunk night he disappeared. I only met him years later.

GEORGE IN HIS HALLOWE'EN COSTUME,
NEW COWBOY BAR, 29/10/93

How can I ~~~~~~~~ ever describe George? He is an alien from a faraway star, a relic from the summer of love still living the life. Brilliant astrologer, drunk, dopehead, uncontrollable, energetic, electric.

Hangover ~~~~~~ mornings in the Rose Garden guesthouse, me chain-smoking, sipping coffee, George spraying half-eaten egg sandwich all over the table and me.

Going out at night, on speed, on vals. I try to chat up girls, George terrorises everybody. He starts exposing himself, dances frenetically. I plead with the bouncers not to kick him out. We reach a compromise. George stops undressing but lets his huge dick hang out of a hole in his stretch pants. I leave with a girl.

After two days George is not back home. I worry, go to look for him in Patpong, find him in his favourite bar (where they let him play his music). He's leaning on an empty beer bottle, barely conscious, his monthly mental disability allowance all spent.

The rest of the month he spends on his roof with his astrological charts. He gives me readings, pacifies himself with incredible amounts of Valium, performs strange rituals, curses me (for not lending him money) and Robert (for being Robert).

George tells the most disgusting stories about sex. But he never had sex during the time I lived with him, only two failed attempts: one Kaosarn Road hooker stole all the money he had saved up for months; a Malaysia Hotel katoey drugged him and stole his money. Of course George accused Robert.

George died and got reborn three days later in a flower pot on Rajadamnern Road. He said in future he had to be more careful with cursing, curses would have a tendency to come back.

George cried when his son sent him a letter.

Life with George, my weird big brother.

GEORGE IN CLIPS II, 19/05/93   GEORGE IN MAXIM'S, 7/11/93

Robert the rat. Ratbert, chess geni-
us, Puerto Rican Jew from New York (maybe the only ████████ member of this▓ mi-
nority). Dreaming of becoming a gangster,
stealing chocolate bars from Seven Eleven.
Peddling AIDS medicine in Soi Cowboy, selling photocopies of his high school diplo-
ma.

I met Robert for the first time in
Kings Lounge, where he saved me from an
angry woman who was about to bottle me. He
became one of my ▓ best friends. The crazy times we spent together I will never
forget, like the night he got titwhipped
off his barstool by a rather large woman I
fancied (having made one tasteless joke too
many). Or when he tried to convince me to
send a kilo of ganja to him in prison ██████
("Everything is sorted out, no problem.
I'll make loads of money, you're not gonna
believe the prices in here"). Or the
Hallowe'en night when he ripped George's
costume off in the middle of Patpong and
left him only with his necklace of lime
green lighters, a red tanga (a present
from George's ██████ platonic love, an Is-
raeli girl who slept with nearly everyone
but George), and a clear plastic bag to
cover his private parts, which kept slipping out of the ████ tight tanga.

George and Robert had a strange love-
hate relationship. The first time George
was sent to immigration prison he accused
Robert of stealing his belongings (as well
as the woman Robert would be cursed with
for the next few years). "You fucking liar,
you even took my ████ green tuxedo coat!"
Robert always said it was the Maori guy
with the burnt face. But one night George
came home crying, saying Robert had barely
escaped a serious beating. "I feel so ▓
sorry for him, his life is so sad!"

Afterwards he always blamed this out-
burst on having been drunk.

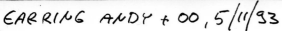

EARRING ANDY + OO, 5/11/93

BRUCE, 26/10/93

Bruce originally came to Bangkok to sort out his heroin habit. He had the perfect ▓▓▓▓ look for Thailand: small, skinny, the smile of an innocent child. Women loved him, and he loved them. As many as possible, often at the same time - which regularly brought him into trouble. Like the time he introduced two women he was having affairs with to each other, and they treated his face with a bottle.

Violence always followed Bruce. Bruce the animal. But he put so much effort into being a part of Thailand. After only a few months he was already fluent in Thai, holding conversations, while the rest of us still struggled with food orders. And for all the luck he had with casual relationships, when he was in love it always left him heartbroken.

Earring Andy is living proof of Murphy's law. Shit happens, and always to Andy. Andy had a great career in Japan, a beautiful fiancée. After a serious mistake at work, he was sent as punishment to Thailand, but still on a good salary, living the high life. Then visa complications set in. He had to get a different visa for his workpermit in Malaysia. In one of the border towns, on a brothel visit, he caught two types of VD. One was cured, the second not recognised. He infected his fiancée. She left him. He lost his job, had to move to a Kaosarn Road shithole. He had to survive as a freelance English teacher. He went ▓▓▓ downhill from then on. He doesn't even like the food in Thailand. Andy's refuge is writing. One day he will write the definitive novel on Bangkok, before Bangkok finishes him.

A BIBLICAL NEW YEAR... SCOTT NEARLY OD'd, THOUGHT HE
BOUGHT COCAINE BUT IT WAS HEROIN. SPENT HOURS
TALKING TO THE WALLS IN VARIOUS BARS.

SCOTT IN TILAC BAR, 31/12/93

'ANDI'S VIEW, 8/2/34

ANDI. 8/2/34

SOME BANGKOK SURVIVAL RULES

① ONLY FOOLS ARE IN FOR LOVE

② BETTER PAY FOR IT, IT'S OFTEN CHEAPER, (BUT FREEBEES ARE ALSO NICE)

③ YOU DON'T LOSE FACE, BUT A WOMAN CAN

④ NEVER, EVER MAKE A WOMAN LOSE FACE

⑤ IF A WOMAN CRIES ON YOUR SHOULDER, GET BOTTLES, GLASSES AND ASHTRAYS OUT OF HER REACH

⑥ DON'T FIGHT - YOU WILL LOSE

⑦ NEVER, EVER FIGHT WITH TUK-TUK DRIVERS

⑧ EXPECT THE UNEXPECTED

⑨ MEKONG WHISKEY IS CHEAP, BUT GIVES THE SHITS

⑩ SMILE!

SOI COWBOY, 28/4/98

NANA PLAZA, SUKHUMVIT SOI 4, 22/5/98

-1- the go-go bar

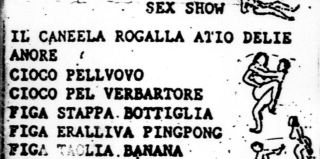

"MASSAGE, MAN, BODY, BODY"

NEIL IN SHADOW, SOI COW BOY, 18/7/97

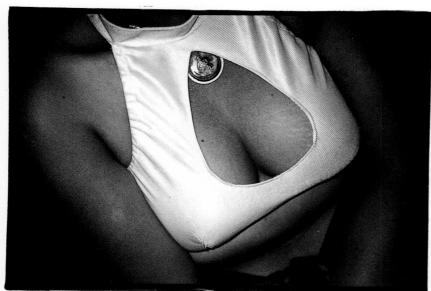

DC-10 BAR, NANA PLAZA, 12/11/96

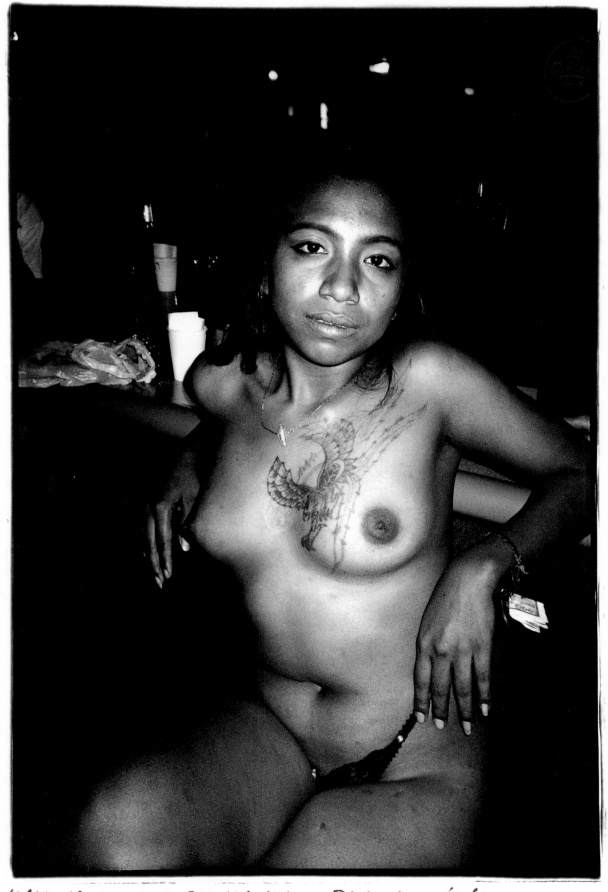

KAY, HOLLYWOOD ROYALE, NANA PLAZA, 23/9/93

WANDEE + BIEM, 8/10/93

WATTANA, 8/10/93

KING'S CASTLE CARNEVAL, PATPONG, 8/10/93

ANN + NIT, 8/10/93

NIT, 8/10/93

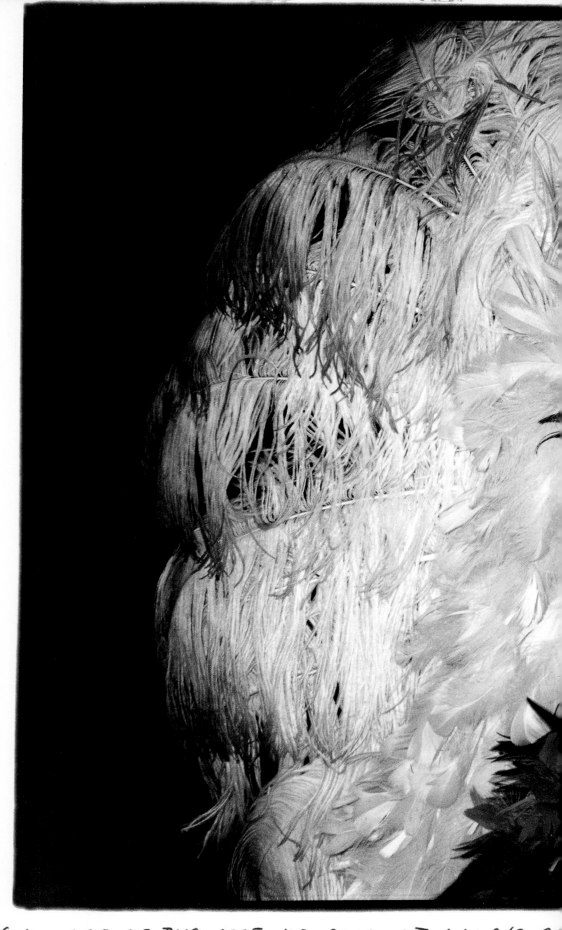

WANDEE, WINNER OF THE COSTUME CONTEST, KING'S CA

CARNEVAL. 8/10/93

☆ Floor 3 ☆

HOLLYWOOD TWO

Wildest Girls & Shows!
☆
Rock'n Roll, Pool & Darts!

HOLLYWOOD STRIP

The Sexiest Girls!
☆
The Most Exciting Shows!
☆
The Only Carousel

Dance Floor in Bangkok!
☆
Huge 100" TV Screen!

Cheapest Drinks – No Cover Charge!
Both open 7:30 till Very Late

NOENG, BIG BLUE, 20/5/98

-2- the blow-job bar

PAT PONG 1, 13/7/97

I2.I0
The Star of Love has opened,
the girls hang around at
the bar. ~~THERE~~ I joke around
with Bhet. Wi comes back
with snacks, listerine and
tissues.

I2.30
Wi plays with the dick of a
grinning guy at the bar.

I2.35
They disappear into~~EN~~ the
back room.

I2.40
Another guy comes in, young,
blond, wide-eyed and open-
mouthed, stuttering that he
wants a beer. The girls
giggle. They send me to another booth, so the guy won't
be so shy.

I2.45
The tout gives the prices.
"The girls can do everything,
everything...!"

I2.55
The first guy is finished,
then the shy one enters the
back room with two girls.

I.20
I'm watching the porn flick,
while another guy comes in
and gets a wank at the bar.

I.25
I leave. The girls in front
of the bar have lunch from
styro-boxes.

SU, IN ROSE BAR, 22/10/93

BUA, IN KANGAROO CLUB, 18/10/93

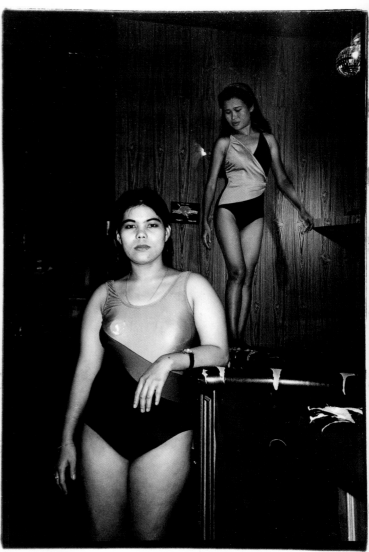

STAR OF LOVE, 5/1/94

KUN + GEOW, STAR OF LOVE, 31/12/93

ADAM + YU, KANGAROO CLUB, 2/12/96

LISTERMINT FOR THE
GIRLS, TO RINSE THE
MOUTH AFTERWARDS
→

THE BUCKET LOADED
WITH SPERM-SOAKED
TISSUES

STAR OF LOVE'S TOILET, 30/10/96

STAR OF LOVE'S BACK ROOM, 13/7/97

LADY NIGHT, 14/2/99

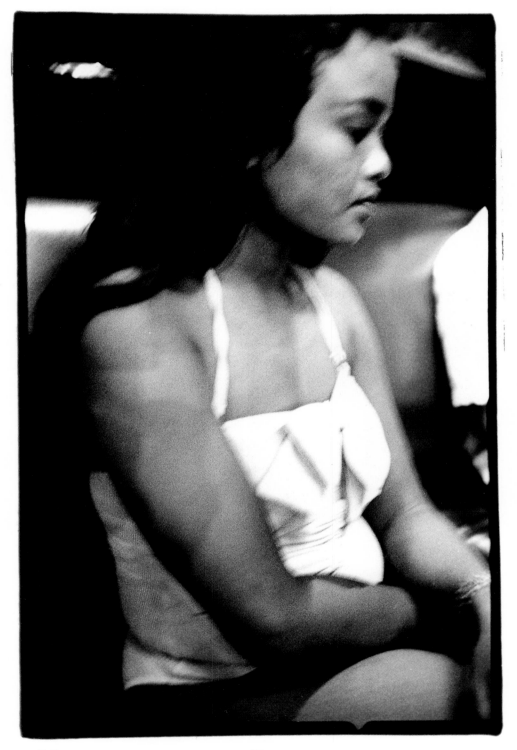

NOC, IN LADY NIGHT.

LADY NIGHT , 6/5/98

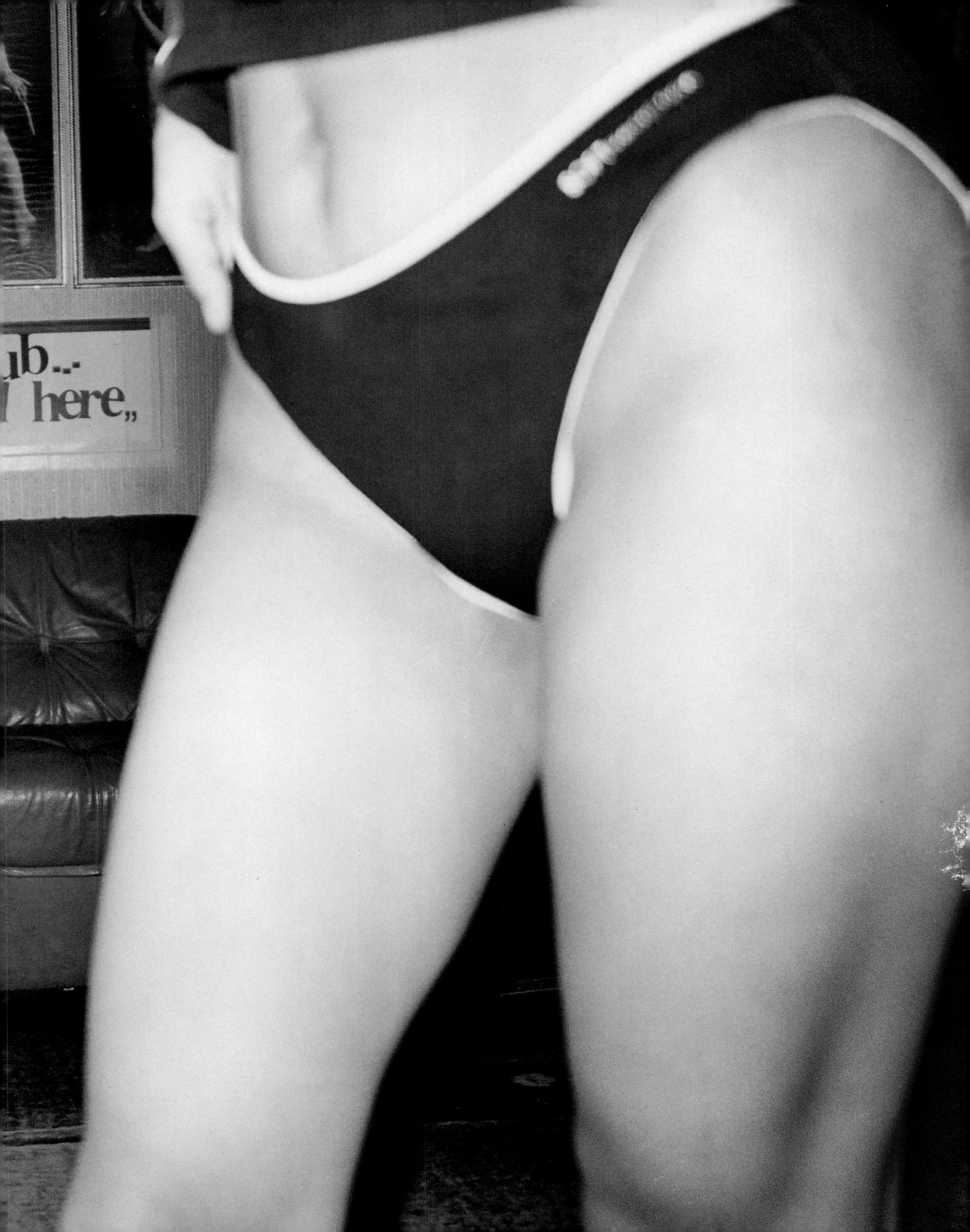
here,

-3- katoey

DIVINE DISCO, SILOM SOI 4, 18/11/96

(KATOEY = TRANSVESTITE, TRANSSEXUAL,)
LADY BOY

DIVINE DISCO BIRTHDAY PARTY + BEAUTY CONTEST, 18/1/96

DIVINE DISCO, 18/1/'96

7/2/96

"I'M NOT MAN,
I'M NOT WOMAN,
I'M AN ANGEL!"

"ROYAL" PARTY AT DJ-STATION, 29/11/98

DJ-STATION, 29/11/98

DJ-STATION, 29/11/98

AFTER THE PARTY, RAMA 4 RD., 29/11/98

AWARD PUB, 15/11/98

IAN'S PARTY, 28/3/97

28/3/97

KING'S LOUNGE, PATPONG, 8/9/93

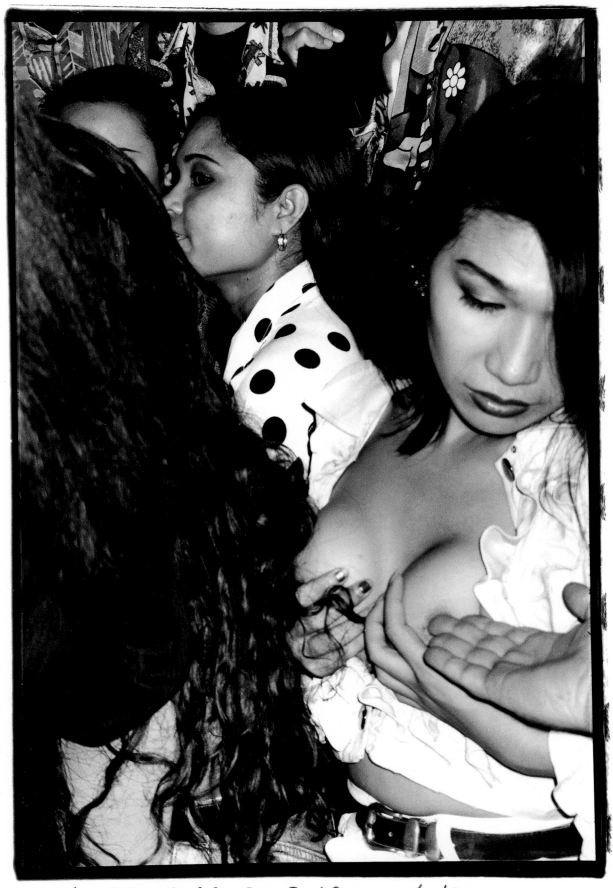

KING'S PARADISE, PATPONG 2, 23/9/93

RIAM, IN KING'S LOUNGE, 15/9/93

GINA, NOW LIVING IN SWITZERLAND, ON A
HOLIDAY IN BANGKOK, KING'S LOUNGE, 23/9/93

THE 24 HOURS BAR, PATPONG 2, 23/7/97

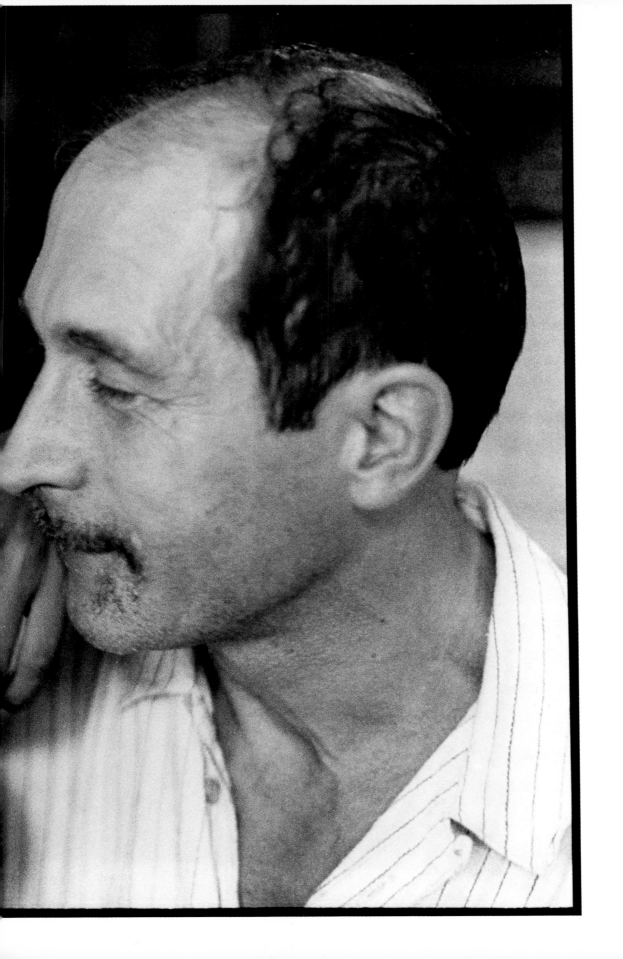

"YOU WANNA FUCK MY ARSE,
'CAUSE I WANNA FUCK YOUR ARSE"

LINDA + ANN, STREET WALKERS ON
RAJADAMNEERN RD., 27/3/94

PEN + JUNG, PATPONG 2, 11/9/93

Suspect Vivat Haewpet (centre) at yesterday's press conference at the Tourist Police second sub-division.

Shun transvestites, tourists told

FOREIGN tourists pursuing forbidden pleasures were yesterday warned by Tourist Police of the dangers of associating with transtistes (katoey).

The warning was issued at a press conference held at the subvision of the Tourist Police Division where a katoey who allegedly drugged and robbed a German tourist was shown to the media.

Pol Col Sanit Meephan, superintendent of the second sub-division, id Vivat Haewpet, 30, was arrest-

ed by Tourist Police at the Rose Town Hotel, on Charan Sanitwong Road, in Thon Buri.

A search of the room reportedly revealed several stolen items and two sleeping pills.

Police said the suspect admitted to mixing sleeping pills in the beer he offered his clients.

When they lost consciousness the suspect allegedly stole their valuables.

The arrest was made within 24 hours of a report filed by Joakim

Clyler, who said that he was drugged at the T.S. Apartment in Arun Amarin Road, Thon Buri.

The German tourist said the crime occurred after he took a katoey to his room on Monday night.

He said when he regained consciousness he discovered that all his cash and valuables worth 54,750 baht were gone.

Police said the suspect had twice been imprisoned and was recently released.

Sauerkraut in a pickle

SIR: A foreign tourist (now a sauerkraut) who was pursuing forbidden pleasures in the Land of Smiles recently got what he deserved — the double whammy — a pill slipping katoey.

The incident was reported in the Bangkok Post which also ran a hilarious picture of this victim "pointing the finger of guilt" at the katoey who allegedly drugged him and then relieved him (not of his pent up masculinity but his cash and valuables worth over 50,000 baht).

The Post reported in glowing detail how the unsuspecting tourist picked up the katoey who he found lurking in the dark and took him/her to his room, either for the purpose or sex or a frank discussion on the significance of Thai pottery dating from the Sukhothai period. You be the judge.

The police, however, should not only be praised for keeping a straight face during the Press Conference, but also for their swift action in netting the suspect within 24 hours of the alleged crime.

The incident also provided the ever vigilant Tourist Police with the opportunity to warn gullible farang tourists like Mr Sauerkraut and his frozen weenie of the dangers of associating with cunning katoeys.

But what if he didn't know it was a katoey? The possibility exists that he was so hypnotised by Asian beauty that he didn't know she was a he.

It's happened before. Remember the after-shave splashed Italian tourist with the gold zodiac chain who unwittingly married a katoey some two years ago.

After wining and dining, courting and consorting with the object of his infatuation, it was only on the wedding night when he groped under the sheet that he discovered his error in judgement and the grand scale of her deception.

As this man now fully understands, katoeys are only capable of deception — not conception.

Micool

The place everybody knows, but nobody talks about except in hints, whispers and smiles. Nobody wants to admit going there, on strange journeys of psychosexual experimentation. Hidden in a quiet corner of hetero bastion Nana Plaza, the katoey bar of Bangkok, the infamous Casanova.

Gender bender, anything goes, chicks with dicks, wild Casanova. Where laws and rules of general sexuality stay out, home of the third sex - not tamed, post-op transsexuals, just the wild angels of Bangkok's night. Proud, aggressive, self-conscious, androgyne, gentle, predatory - and so sexual.

Casanova is representative of Bangkok's weirdness: a secret of limitless possibilities, pushing the borders of human sexuality, XXXX its moral foundations. Existentially so disturbing: Who am I? I define myself through my gender, through my XXXXXXXXX attraction to the opposite (or the same)sex. But people here, what is their gender? How do I define myself now?

The ultimate XXX experience of self. In Casanova the only escape is not to enter. No voyeurism is possible, there is no woman in whose arms you can hide. You will be thrown in, left to deal with yourself. Any way you can.

YUYI, 5/3/98

NOI, 8/6/98

JANE, 5/3/98

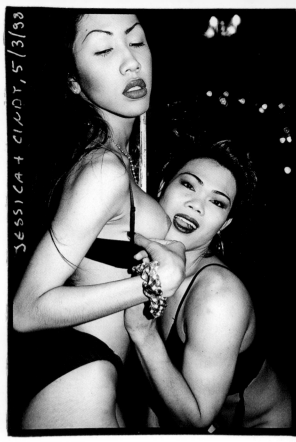

JESSICA + CINDY, 5/3/98

JESSICA + CINDY, 5/3/98

NOI, 4/8/98

NUI + JESSICA

5/3/98

JANE, 4/8/98

MARSHA, 5/3/98

CINDY, 20/12/96

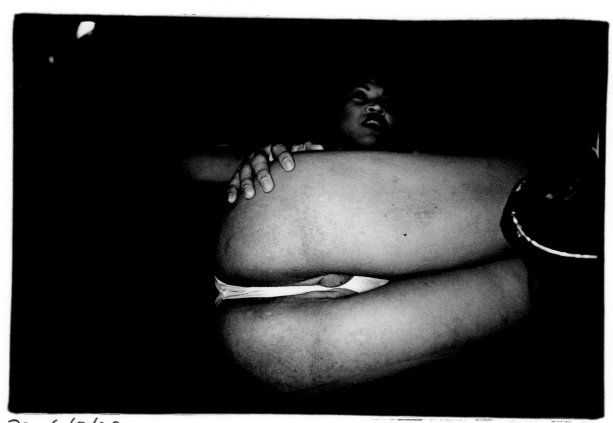

PO, 4/8/98

-4- the disco

KING'S LOUNGE, PATPONG, 23/7/97

KAY, IN KING'S LOUNGE, 1/11/93

NAAM, IN KING'S LOUNGE, 26/10/93

OH, IN PEPPERMINT CLUB, 10/12/93

MEE, IN KING'S LOUNGE, 18/9/93

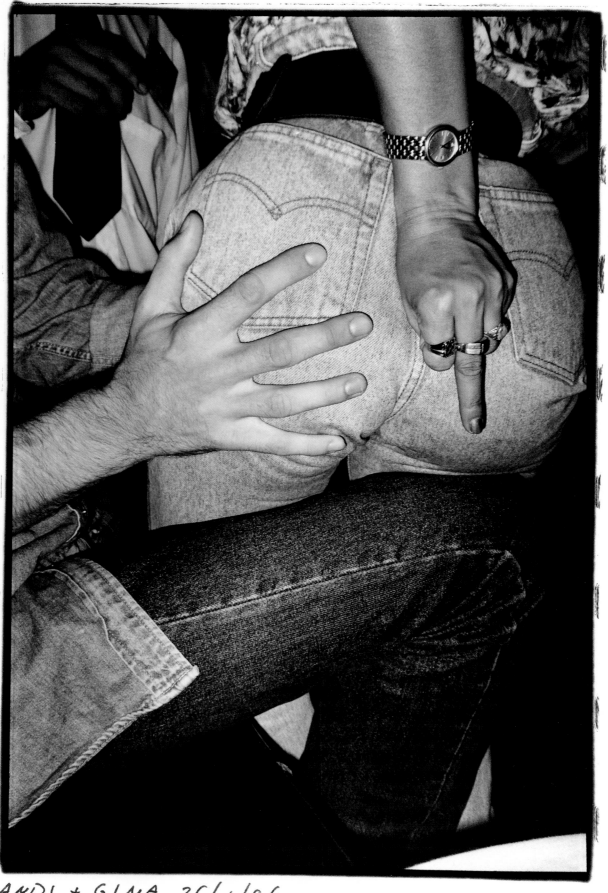

ANDI + GINA, 26/1/94

AEH + ME, KING'S LOUNGE, 6/10/93

TOY+TOON, 28/9/93

4/11/93

LEILA+GAY+TOY

POLAROID KEEPS YOU IN THE PICTURE

TOON, 28/9/93

TOY, 6/10/93

11/10/93

JEFF+GEORGE

18/12/93

KING'S PALACE, 15/11/98

KING'S LOUNGE WAITERS

KING'S LOUNGE 9/12/93

UDOM, BOUNCER, 18/3/93

KING'S LOUNGE

MANDI, 10/12/93

BIG BILL, 14/3/93

KING'S LOUNGE WAITERS

18/12/93

14/3/93

•5- the street

TUK-TUK, SILOM, 17/12/96

Nobody wants to be on the street. The street is hostile
territory, to your health, your nerves. Endless traffic jams,
air thick enough to cut with a knife, blaring noise of two-
stroke-engined motorcycles, the fear of being run over by che-
mically-hyped bus and lorry drivers.

Moving along the street wrecks your nerves. Standing in
overcrowded buses, watching the taxi meter climb, stuck in
traffic, risking limbs on the back of a motorcycle taxi.

SUKHUMVIT RD.,

Daily Bangkok rush hour horror. Starts at 6 in the morning. Ends at II at night.

The street is for the cazy and the beggars, the homeless and the dog packs; and, a little way up the social ladder, for up-country migrant labourers, street walkers and traffic policemen, whose destroyed lungs force them to retire by the age of DSSS foりrty.

TAXI TEMPLE, 20/10/96

THE GARLAND SELLER

BIAOW, THE SWEETEST STREET DOG EVER, 9/2/94
(HER NAME MEANS "BENT". WHEN SHE WAS
A PUPPY, A CAR HIT HER. SINCE THEN
HER HEAD WAS OUT OF SHAPE. FOR MANY
YEARS SHE LIVED IN FRONT OF MY BANG-
LAMPOO GUESTHOUSE).

BABY ELEPHANT ON SUKHUMVIT ROAD

ISAARN CONSTRUCTION WORKERS,
ASOKE/SUKHUMVIT, 18/12/93

SUKHUMVIT, 5/1/94

JOY+KHAO, HER ADOPTED DOG, ON A
SMALL LAWN NEAR PINKLAO BRIDGE, 5/11/93

KEN SEE, SUKHUMVIT RD., 31/12/93

BUS Nº 2, 30/12/93

RAMA 4 RD., 29/4/97

TUAN, SILOM RD, 12/2/94

ANUSAK, WAITING TO DIE, RAJADAM-
NERN RD., 3/2/94

"DO YOU WANT A CIGARETTE?"
"NO."
"MONEY?"
"NO. BUT PLEASE CAN YOU KILL
 ME. I CAN'T DO IT MYSELF, I
BELIEVE IN BUDDHA."

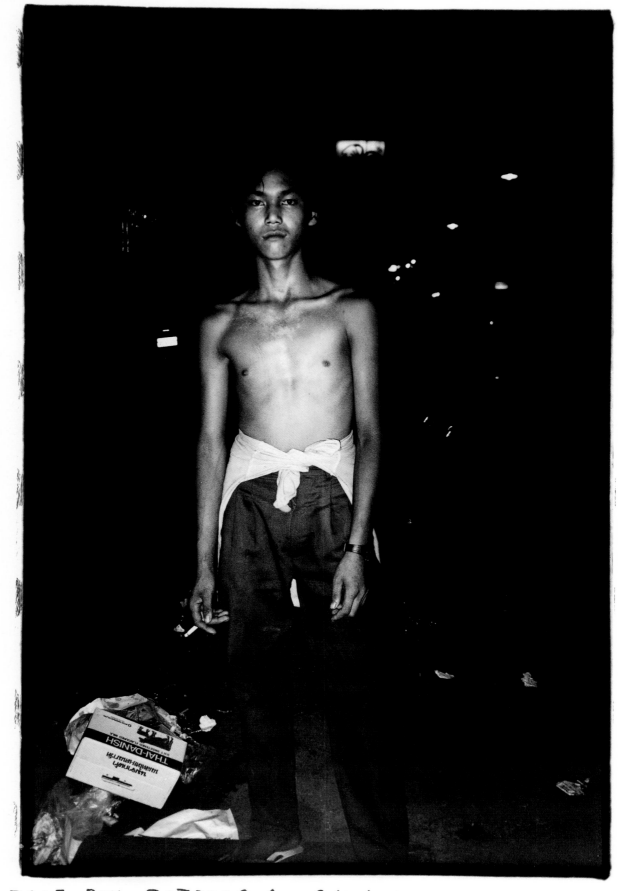

DEAF BOY, PATPONG 1, 8/9/93

"HELLO, HELLO ! ! COME WIT' YOU, WHERE YOU STAY ?"

SU, AT THE SOUTHERN BUS TERMINAL, SNIFFING GLUE
28/6/97

DON FEELS LIKE SHIVA, SUKHUMVIT ROAD, 22/10/96

FUCKED UP, KING'S PARADISE, PAT PONG, 20/9/93

AFTER DOING TOO MANY DRUGS ON THE ISLANDS, THIS
GUY CAME UP TO BANGKOK, AND FAST EARNED HIM-
SELF A BAD REPUTATION: BIG, MEAN, ALWAYS
FIGHTING, HYPER AGGRO. PEOPLE SAID HE HAD ONCE
BEEN NICE AND FUNNY. ONE OF THE VERY FEW
TIMES I HAD TROUBLE IN THE NIGHTLIFE WAS WHEN
HE TRIED TO PICK A FIGHT WITH ME IN KING'S
LOUNGE FOR NO REASON. THE ONLY THING THAT
SAVED ME FROM A SERIOUS BEATING WAS THAT
I WAS ON GOOD TERMS WITH THE BOUNCERS,
WHO JUMPED IN STRAIGHT AWAY. THE RUMOUR
IS THAT A FEW MONTHS LATER HE WAS FOUND
WITH A BULLET IN HIS HEAD ON A BEACH IN
KO PAN NGAN.

MANOD + DEN, SAPHAN KWAI, 22/11/98

UNDER THE SATHORN FLYOVER

SUKHUMVIT RD., 10/1/94

-6- thermae/ the family

EVE, AT THE BEERSTALL IN FRONT OF THERMAE
18/7/97

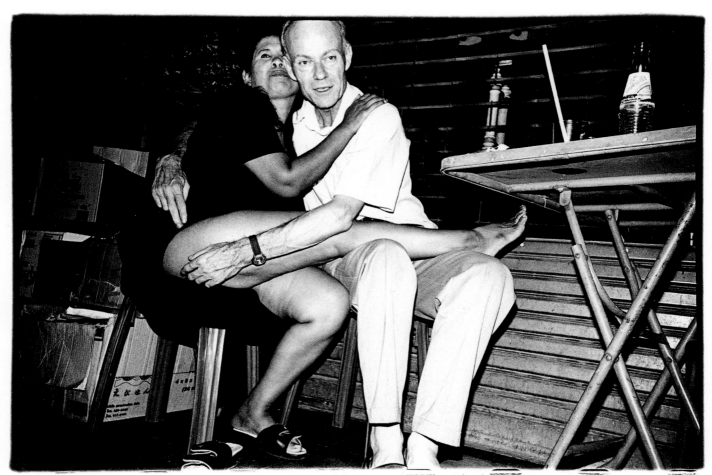

DAVID + NOI, 7/11/99

DAVID SAYS:

"FUCK THE WEST! WHEN
WE GET ON THE PLANE...
WE JUST COME HERE TO
GET AWAY."

"YOU WANT I ONLY GO WIT' YOU?! YOU DON' UNDERSTAN'!
WE HERE 'CAUSE WE LIKE BUTTERFLY, ALL OF US,
EVERY BODY. O.K.?"

AT THE JUKEBOX, 13/12/93

TUKATA , 26/12/93   JEFF, 2/2/94

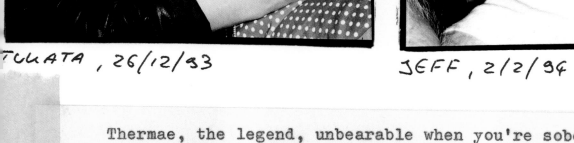

    Thermae, the legend, unbearable when you're sober, paradise
when pissed. The temple of Hedonism, epicentre of Bangkok's
nightlife, a bar from a different universe, a different time.
    Diplomats and English teachers, scam artists and spies, oil
men, old hookers, young hookers, deaf hookers, secretaries and
sales girls a bit short at the end of the month, students and
housewives.
    A crowd, moving, chatting, laughing, hunting, kissing till
the blue of the morning. Screwing, sleeping, working. Another
night.
    Growing old with Thermae. Arriving, waking up suddenly twen-

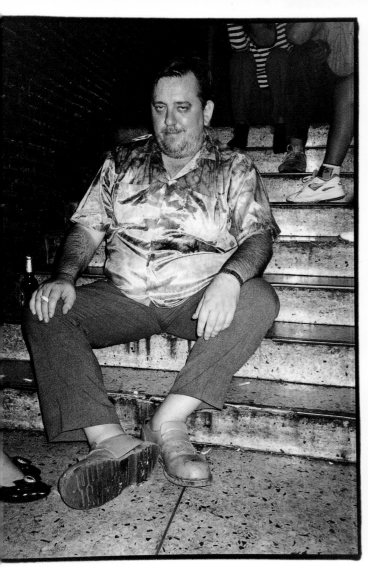 

MEINARD, 13/2/94
   (MANY YEARS AGO, MEINARD AND DAENG
      WERE A COUPLE)

ty years later, still at the same endless party.

   Into the dark courtyard, entering through a small door, walking past the toilets (lasses doing their make up, the incredible
transformation of a plain Isaarn girl into a Thermae star), down
a steep stairway lined with the first preying eyes. Inside. A
low-roofed neon-lit cave, no décor, just the juke box, a bar, a
few tables and chairs, black naugahide sofas grouped along the
walls in niches.

   Minimalism, the whole Bangkok night scene naked with no
colors, no masks.

NAN, 13/12/93

"SOMETIMES I LOOK AROUND, AND I JUST DON'T REMEMBER, WITH WHICH GIRL I WENT, AND WITH WHOM I DIDN'T."

THERMAE FAREWELL PARTY, 16/7/97

DAEM + TUK, 5/1/94

PAUL + THE COP, 14/7/96

MEM + EM, 26/3/94

AT THE JUGE BOX, 14/7/96

The party's over at the Thermae

by John Hail

AN expatriate institution for 30 years, the Thermae Coffee Shop closes its doors for the last time tomorrow.

During the Vietnam War, it vied for the title of favourite GI bar with such legendary late-night haunts as the Thai Yonok and Grace Hotel.

Only the Thermae survived Bangkok's frenzied modernisation and building boom relatively unchanged. But a wrecking crew will get to work tomorrow after the tacky furnishings and fittings that supported the Thermae's distinctly Thai floating world are carted away.

Seven nights a week, barring most coups and holidays, the Thermae was packed with mainly Western men and mainly northeastern women from midnight through to the wee hours.

Their intercultural interaction varied from a short-time to a lifetime.

There are no statistics on how many marriages began with a furtive glance or grope at the Thermae. But there can be no doubt that the crowded, subterranean coffee shop on the Sukhumvit Road tourist belt was the birthplace for a large number of romantic liaisons.

Norman Smith, 54, a long-time American resident of Thailand, said: "The first time I dropped down to the Thermae was in 1967 and most of the customers were GIs.

"In those days there was a lot of rivalry between the services, mostly between the marines and the army, so there were lots of fights."

Intense rivalry also existed between the American servicemen on rest and recreation visits from Vietnam and the more 50,000 GIs based in Thailand, referred to derisively by the combat veterans as Bangkok Warriors.

"After the bars closed, the Thermae would fill up with GIs and a few civilians," Mr Smith said. "The juke box played the song *San Francisco* over and over. The girls from the massage parlour upstairs drifted down in their pink hot pants. It was great."

Another favourite on the juke box, James Brown's *America's the Greatest Country in the World*, was the catalyst for a refurbishment that saw the Thermae close briefly in 1969. Australian servicemen, tired of hearing the soul number, clashed with their American comrades and wrecked the joint. When the Thermae reopened after a week, America might still have been the greatest country in the world, but not on the Thermae juke box.

The name Thermae is of Greek origin, a kind of bath house where people gathered to discuss the issues of the day.

Thermae was said to have sold more beer, mainly Singha, than any other outlet in Thailand.

High volume, and it was whispered, first-rate police connections, made the Thermae resistant, but not immune, to periodic police crackdowns and coups.

Post-coup curfews would generally push the Thermae's prime time back a few hours. Then, as the midnight hour approached, a mating frenzy would sweep the coffee shop.

Those who managed to pair in time would then have to deal with the taxi drivers whose greed knew no bounds in the countdown to curfew.

The Thermae survived by bending with the prevailing political and economic winds. When the GIs pulled out in 1976, the vacuum was filled by a surge of European sex tourists and waves of youthful back-packers.

The Thermae partied on.

Christopher Moore, a Bangkok-based Canadian novelist, found inspiration in the Thermae for a series of novels. In *A Killing Smile,* the thinly disguised Thermae is called headquarters.

Like many of the Thermae's old hands, Mr Moore mourned the closing of headquarters as the end of an era.

"The Thermae was the perfect crossroads where people of all nationalities dropped into the underworld, the nightworld," Mr Moore said. "No one was excluded. Old hands. New hands. People with no hands. The Thermae was the ultimate party, a celebration of conversation, local gossip, travellers' information and of course, there were the women."

The Thermae women, have, in general, accepted the nightspot's imminent destruction more philosophically, with a *mai pen rai.*

A 25-year distaff veteran of the Thermae said: "We only came here because the coffee was cheaper than at the Grace, the Nana and the Thai Yonok. "There will always be another place."

Indeed, a new Thermae, in a basement a couple of doors up Sukhumvit Road is scheduled to open on Tuesday.

A Thermae waiter lamented: "I'm sorry we have to close but what can I do? They want to build a condo or something. Come to the new place. It will be just the same."

But old Thermae hands already have started complaining it's just not the same. — UPI

JOHN, NIGHTLIFE VETERAN, THE REAL LIFE "A.K. SNOW" IN CHRISTOPHER MOORE'S BANGKOK NOVELS. JOHN HAS THE GREATEST HAWAIIAN SHIRT COLLECTION IN THAILAND.

THE PARTY GOES ON, THE NEW THERMAE, 11/9/98

ARNOLD, 15/2/99

PAA, IN A SHORTTIME HOTEL NEAR THE GRAND PALACE.
22/12/93

NING AND HER "BOY FRIEND" BAN, GLONG ROT, 26/3/94

PATTAYA

Vice blitz backfires as cop spends night with woman

The woman charged with stealing his car

Pattaya, Reuters

A policeman assigned to the Pattaya vice purge was relieved of his car and gun by a woman he had spent the night with in a short-time hotel.

A woman was later charged with stealing the car, gun, mobile phone and other valuables from Pol Pvt Itthiphol Warayu as he slept.

Pvt Itthiphol, a member of a task force sent to Pattaya a week ago to crack down on vice, had met the woman on Wednesday night.

A police officer said: "The suspect said she had just driven the car around to show her friends, but Itthiphol insisted that she meant to steal from him so we had to detain her."

In another incident related to the red light purge, several people, including children, were hurt when a Crime Suppression Division patrol car, apparently driven by a drunken policeman, slammed into the rear of a sedan at a traffic light in Pattaya.

The impact of the collision by the speeding police BMW shunted the car into the rear of two others that had stopped at the red light.

Hundreds of police have been sent to Pattaya after Prime Minister Chavalit Yongchaiyudh declared it a "dirty town" following repeated reports of widespread drug abuse and organised crime groups who prey mainly on tourists.

Pattaya police frequently receive complaints of women drugging and robbing tourists who often come to Pattaya for its sex industry.

DEAF GIRL, IN A SMALL KLONG ROD
BROTHEL, 29/1/94

WAN, 13/1/94

BOM, LLONG ROT, 26/3/94

t home (asia paradiso)

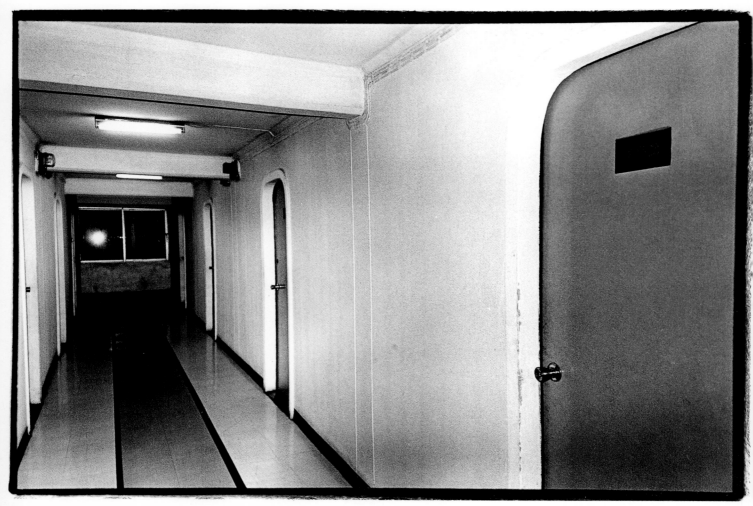

THE NARAI APARTMENT, SUKHUMVIT ROAD, 2/9/98

BRUC

TOM + ANDY, AFTER WORK, 19/1/94

The more hair I lose
The more head I get

PATPONG GEORGE, NOW RETIRED
FROM THE WILD LIFE

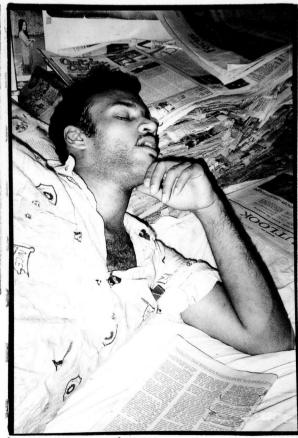

ROBERT, 3/4/94

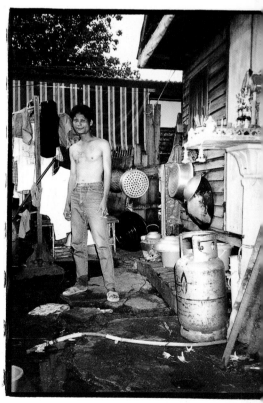

NAN IN HER SCUM HUT, 13/12/93
THIS SCUM COMPOUND, UNDER A HIGH-
RISE NEAR LUMPINI PARK, IS SHARED
BY SEVERAL GENERATIONS OF THER-
MAE HOOKERS AND THEIR THAI BOY-
FRIENDS. MOST ROOMS ARE OCCUPIED IN SHIFTS,
DAYTIME FOR NIGHT WORKERS, NIGHT TIME FOR
DAY WORKERS.

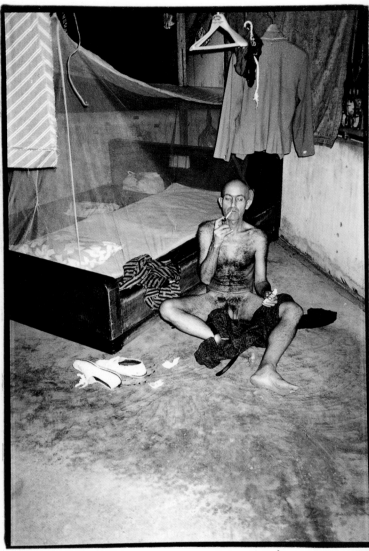

SCOTT, 1/7/97
(JUST THINKING OF GOING
TO AN AA MEETING)

GEORGE ON HIS ROOF, 4/10/93
HE MADE HIS HOME ON THE
ROOF OF THE ROSE GARDEN
GUEST HOUSE, 30 DOLLARS A
MONTH. HIS BED ALWAYS
ORIENTED TOWARDS ASTRO-
LOGICAL CONFIGURATIONS.
A FEW MONTHS LATER GEORGE
WAS KICKED OUT FOR MA-
KING A HUGE EXPLOSION
(NOT THE FIRST TIME HE SET
FIRE TO A GUEST HOUSE HE
WAS LIVING IN).

JEFF, IN KENNY'S GUEST HOUSE, 2/11/98
JEFF WAS JUST BACK AFTER A FEW MONTHS
IN A MONASTERY. THIS WAS THE FIRST
TIME WE MET SINCE HE DISAPPEARED
NEARLY 5 YEARS EARLIER

EARRING ANDY, 2/3/98
  ANDY NOW LIVES WITH A WIFE HE
DOESN'T PARTICULARLY LOVE, AND HIS
THREE CHILDREN. HE STILL DREAMS OF
RETURNING TO JAPAN.

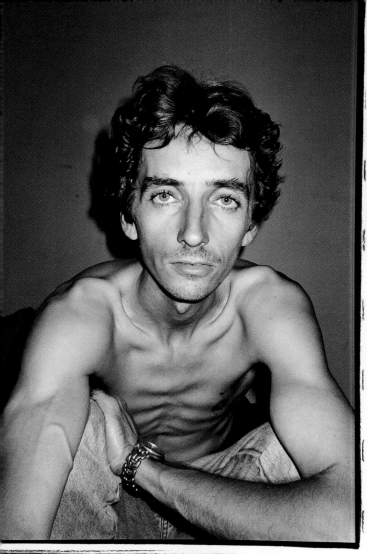

IAN'S CEREMONY, PHNOM PENH
20/2/94

Ian is how I imagine William
Burroughs when he was young: incre-
dibly intense, hungry for life,"For
as long as I can remember I have been
fascinated by the needle, the powder,
and the ritual of shooting up. I am
a junky. I always was and will be."
I went on a visa run to Cambodia, in
the crazy, lawless days just afterm
UNTAC left. A few wild days, stoned
out of my head.

    Me and Ian clicked right away. I
think he was the most uncompromising
person I have ever met. He liked my
attitude towards photography and asked me to take some photos of him
while he was shooting up.

    The last I heard of Ian was that
he left Cambodia two years later,
when he discovered he had AIDS.

THE NAM WAH HOTEL, PENANG. OUR VISA RUN
ROUTINE, EVERY THREE MONTHS (IF YOU
STILL CARED)

SUNSET AT DAVID'S APARTMENT

Living in Bangkok is a cons-
tant journey at the edge of mad-
ness. There is something in the
air fuelled by the heat, the
traffic, the ~~madang anonmity~~ *anonymity*. It
drives people to do things they
would never do anywhere else. You
can do anything you want, be whatever you dreamt of being, go to
any extreme.

Borderlines you only see
when you've crossed them - same
for everyone in this city of
illusions.

-9- Bangkok for life

JOURNEY TO THE PRESENT

Life was always too narrow for me in Germany. Since
I can remember I wanted to be somebody else, live
somewhere else. I got kicked out of schools, threw
stones in demonstrations, did drugs. Nothing made
me happy. Always searching for something.

I thought I found the answer when I went to India for the first time. It opened a new world for
me, full of questions. A freedom I had always been
looking for, no rules or regulations but my own, no
expectations, just to be.

In Germany I knew my future would have been
university, jobs, family. Suicide.

So I barely finished school, worked nightshifts
for two months, then left. with a few intervals I
travelled for the next five years. Walking Hindu
pilgrimages in the Himalayas, surfing in Indonesia's
islands, getting lost on India's plains, sipping
tea in China's mountains, chewing kat in Djibouti's
slums, attending timeless ceremonies in Tibet. What
a life, just caring for the present ~~present~~ moment.

But I became restless and lonely. Until I found
Bangkok. All my friends carried some sort of load
on their backs. In Bangkok there was no need to
hide it, it was accepted, even expected. We fucked
up, life fucked us, so we fucked life, and had
loads of fun with it.

Because bad things had happened to us we ░░░░░░ thought we could behave the way we did. But bad ░░░░ things happen to everyone, so that was no reason. In truth it was just coincidence: right time, right place, right state of mind.

We were so naive, and had no idea that serious things were waiting to happen. We came from all backgrounds, some of us had no education, most had left careers behind. We went out together, shared women. And Bangkok's night became our prison. We were addicted to the lifestyle, slaves to it; intoxicated by a moral set-up incomprehensible and alien to anyone outside the scene. And in turn we couldn't understand other people anymore, their bigotry, their double standards, trapped as we were in our bubble of illusions.

Many of us have left, some have been or still are in jail, a consequence of the life we chose. Most of us have created some sort of life for ourselves here in Thailand.

Bangkok has changed our lives so profoundly it will never leave us. Whatever we do, our experience of Bangkok will remain. We just have to come to terms with it. Somehow.

NIAS '89, SURFING, TRIPPING, SURFING

SRI LANKA '83/30

SUMATRA '89, MY FIRST TIME
AT THE EQUATOR

SUMATRA '89

INDIA '88, BORN AGAIN!

DJIBOUTI '90

THE IRANIAN DESERT '92

MAGIC HIMALAYA '91

ABOVE THE SPRING OF THE GANGES

SOME WHERE IN THE INDIAN
OCEAN '90

NANG, 9/91

WITH NANG I HAD MY FIRST GLIMPSE INTO THE STRANGE NIGHT LIFE, THE BANGKOK PARADOX. I HAD JUST COME FROM INDIA, ON THE WAY TO INDONESIA. AFTER A FEW SEXLESS MONTHS BANGKOK'S GO-GO BARS WERE HEAVEN. I MET HER ON THE FIRST NIGHT. WE FIXED A MEETING FOR THE NEXT AFTERNOON. WE WENT TO HER PLACE AND FUCKED LIKE RABBITS. THE NEXT MORNING I ASKED HER HOW MUCH SHE WANTED. SHE SAID SHE WANTED NO MONEY FROM ME, SHE WANTED ME TO STAY WITH HER. I THOUGHT, "COOL", STAYED A FEW DAYS, THEN TRAVELLED ON. SHE CRIED, SAID SHE LOVED ME.

SOMETIME LATER I CAME BACK. WITHIN TWO WEEKS SHE DROVE ME CRAZY. WE STILL FUCKED, BUT AT THE SAME TIME SHE WAS FUCKING TWO OTHER GUYS FOR MONEY, AND I DON'T KNOW HOW MANY SHORT TIMES. WHEN I TOLD HER IT WAS OVER, SHE THREW A SCENE AND WENT NUTS. A FEW YEARS LATER I MET HER AGAIN. SHE HAD MADE IT: LOADS OF MONEY, REGULAR TRIPS AROUND THE WORLD, LAND, A HOUSE AND CAR IN HER VILLAGE.

SHE STILL INSISTED THAT SHE LOVED ME.

JOY ASKED ME, "ARE YOU SCARED OF AIDS?" I SAID, "I USE CONDOMS, AND IF I STILL GET IT, FUCK IT." SHE SAID, "GOOD, BECAUSE I HAVE IT. THIS IS MY LAST NIGHT, TOMORROW I GO BACK TO MY VILLAGE."

WHAT PUZZLES ME STILL TODAY IS THAT I WASN'T SCARED, I JUST SAW IT AS A CHALLENGE, LIKE AN, "I DON'T GIVE A FUCK, I'M IN BANGKOK" INITIATION. SEX WITH HER WAS LIKE A BATTLE. I PUT ON A CONDOM. FIRST CHANCE, SHE RIPPED IT OFF, SO I PUT ON ANOTHER ONE. I SLEPT, THEN WOKE UP TO FIND HER LOWERING HERSELF ON ME, AND WAS BARELY ABLE TO SLIP THE RUBBER ON. OVER AND OVER AGAIN. IN THE END I GAVE IN, CAME INSIDE HER BARE-BACKED. IN THE MORNING SHE SAID SHE WAS JUST JOKING. WHO KNOWS? ANYHOW, I WAS MORE SCARED OF ONE OF THOSE HYPER-RESISTANT VDs THAT CAN KEEP YOU OFF THE GAME FOR MONTHS.

THE FEAR CAME A LONG TIME AFTER, WHEN I CAME TO MY SENSES AND HAD THE TEST. THREE TORTURED DAYS WAITING FOR MY RESULT. NEGATIVE. NEVER AGAIN.

Joy, 30/10/93

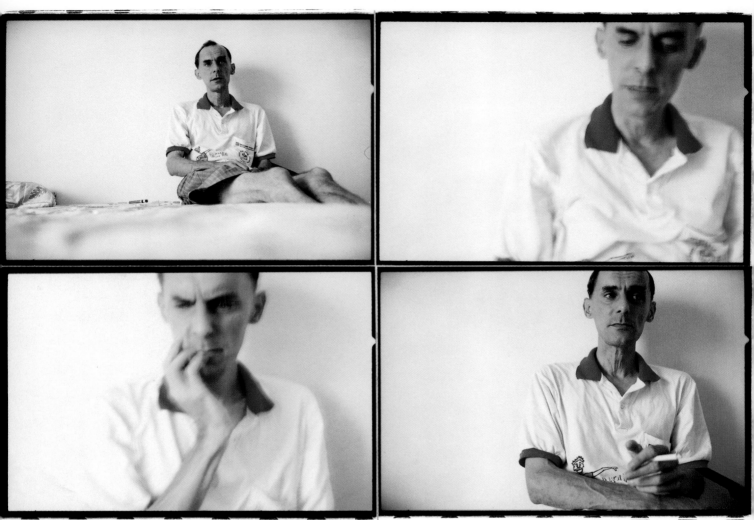

SCOTT, 17/9/98

-What first brought you to Asia?

-I had never been to Asia before. I was unemployed. I had money
saved. A very good friend of mine had been here and we were just
talking about Asia, the various countries, working in different
places. He suggested teaching. I had thought about teaching in
America, but at the time - it was '92 - there wasn't much work
in California. My friend and I were looking for work in Los Angeles, and couldn't find any. I was actually thinking of stay-
ing in Los Angeles, but I made the decision to come over here.
D I had money saved, but as the weeks went by the money was ₨₨₨₨
getting lower and lower living in Los Angeles trying to find
work, so I finally decided just to get up and go.

-Why Asia? Why nŏt Mexico or Europe?

-Well, I had visited Europe already, and wasn't too interested.

-I could have gone to South America, could have gone to Mexico.
My friend had travelled around the world, and he told me Thailand was his favourite country.

-For what reason?

-When he was here, in '86, he said that the people here were the
friendliest people he had met.

-How long was he here?

-Only about a month. I said OK, I will try it, but the original
plan was not to stay. I thought I would travel around Asia, and
if I didn't like it I would just go back to America. It wasn't
clear what I was going to do, so I just packed and left, that
was it.

-Was Bangkok your first destination in Asia?

-Bangkok was the first place; I flew straight to Bangkok.

-So did you basically get stuck here? Since then have you been to
any other country in Asia?

-No, I haven't been anywhere elseǝ. I did the tourist thing. I

got here, went up north, then down south to the islands. Actually,
I hated Bangkok when I first came here. I was only here for three
days, and I hated it. I got down to the islands, Ko Samui, stayed
too long, spent all my money, so I decided to come up to Bangkok
and find work. It had to be worth a try.

-Saving up money to go somewhere else?

-Yes. Of course that didn't happen. In fact the only other country
I have been into is Malaysia, to renew my visa, and that's it.
It's funny actually, thinking back. I don't even know why
I stayed in Bangkok, but I started really liking it, I enjoyed
the free spirit thing. Working, not the nine-to-five routine,
working your own hours and going out at night with friends...

-The whole bar scene...?

-Yeah.

-You get this illusion, don't you? It seems so free...

-You really get that impression. But also, I met a lot of nice
people, other foreigners. And that's why I stayed in Bangkok so
long, it's the relationships with people from all over.

-What did you think about Asia before you came here? Does that
match your experiences here?

-I hadn't given Asia that much thought. I always loved to travel,
it didn't matter if it were Asia, Europe or Mexico. I loved to
travel; I travelled a lot around America. I always had that in
me, to go to places. But my perception of Asia was really limi-
ted, which I think is the case for most Americans. And as far
as Thailand is concerned, a lot of people assume you came over
here for the girls, but I didn't. I didn't think about girls
that much. I mean I had heard a few things, but in truth my
friend who had been here, he never even bothered with the girls.
It wasn't because of the girls. But on the other hand I must say,
when I did get here, I did immediately - so typical - fall in
love with all these girls. I thought they were just gorgeous.
The time I lived in San Francisco bay area you didn't see Thai

people that much. You'd see Filipinos or Japanese, and Chinese.
There is something about the Thai face, that old Siamese look.
-Might that have been only that put-on look, the so-called "Thai
smile"?
-There is something to be said for "the land of smiles". I mean,
we joke about that, but in a way it's also true, there is an
attraction to it when you come from a western country, where
people are more serious. And this idea of"sanook", to have fun
for fun's sake, it's a real nice idea when you come from America,
where it's hard to have fun. At first you are under the illusion.
I think a part of that for me was going down to the islands, having that sort of"island fever", you're out all night, partying,
meeting girls. Time means nothing. There were two things that
really stuck me being an American: time was not important and I
really felt, and I still do even today, safe in terms of ▒▒▒▒
crime. You are looking over your shoulder a lot in America; the
crime is there. And to come here, there were so many times, when
I was drunk at night, yet nobody ever bothered me. I still feel
that to a certain extent, but of course things have changed. I
mean, I see the reality of Thailand. Of course it's not that safe,
but compared to my country, it's a lot safer.
-If you knew before coming to Thailand, you would be around girls
and all that... What did you imagine?
-We were pretty naive about that kind of thing. ▒▒▒▒ We fell into
a... I guess it's a trap in a way. The Tourist ▒▒▒▒▒▒ Authority
has these big posters in America of "exotic Thailand" and you
actually do believe that. Now of course I know different.
-Did the reality of the sex business surprise you?
-I was surprised about Thai men - once I found out that there are
also areas for Thai men and this has been going on for longer.
You might think that it's only foreigners, but you come to realise
it's virtually all men.
-So you basically adapted to Thailand?

-Well, that's the Thai way, isn't it, if you are a man? And the
idea that the father introduces his son to a brothel, to lose
his virginity, that's very common. Another thing I didn't realise was how common it is to have minor ▓▓▓▓ wives. And how much
your status goes up the more money, the more wives you have. I
began to see how many men have minor wives. And it's even accepted by some women. That's changing now, but a lot of women just
accepted that. The primary wife gets the house and all that ▓
goes with it but the minor wives also have apartments where their
husbands can go visit them.
-About you and Thailand. How have you changed in the four and a
half years since you arrived?
-I certainly did not think I would still be here. I have adapted
in a way, living here I'm more patient than I used to be about life in general. I don't know, maybe Thai ways could have done that
to me. I'm not as serious as I was -or at least not as aggressive,
which has more to do with American culture. So I'm more patient
and I tend to have a little more fun.
-But having ▓▓▓▓▓▓▓ no money, living day by day?
-That's interesting. I just took up that attitude and said "I'm
just like the Thais, I'm gonna live day by day", which usually
means having no money, because you're goin' out and you don't
care what's gonna happen the next day.h   j
-Did you ever live like that in America?
-Not really, you really can't. I saved money in America, the mind-
set is different.
-Is it a healthy way of life in the end?
-No, in the end it's not. It sounds good for a while, but you
can't really do that. And the thing is, it also has to do with
my age. I mean if you are twenty, OK, maybe your family helps
you out, but when you are where I am now, over forty, It's too
difficult. You really have to think about the future a little
bit, have a plan, something.

-At the moment, can you think of any plan you might have for the future? Teaching English here, this line of work doesn't have much of a future.

-The only way I can do what I do... And I still, even to this day, like to teach. I still enjoy it. I was thinking yesterday, because I am teaching some big classes now and I enjoy that, I have to get serious. Maybe find work at an international school, an actual career with all the benefits. That's where I have to get serious. I really wanna do that.

-What's the worst experience you have had here in Thailand?

-I would say two things. One was going to prison, and the other was falling in love with a Thai girl.

-Tell me about the love first.

-Yeah; that's one thing I have grown a lot more cynical about, but at the time I just fell for a prostitute, like a lot of guys. I was very naive, believing she would always be around and, as a lot do, she just vanished one day and broke my heart. I was really hurt. I had been here maybe two years, and had not really been involved with any girl. And I did get involved with her, and I would really miss her when she wasn't around. And then she just vanished; I was really hurt by that. The worst part of all that was - is - that you get more jaded, more cynical about those kind of things. And that actually hurt me a lot for a while. I used to go down to Thermae and look for her. I didn't want to be bothered by any other girl, I just sat there looking for her, because I didn't know where she was.

-Did she say anything to you... did she have relationships with other guys at the same time?

-I would imagine, probably yes. She would be away a week, and then she would come back. But I was led to believe she might have really cared about me. She would phone me to see how I was, come over to see me. And it wasn't all money by the way, either.

-Do you know why she left you?

-Yeah, I did find out, when I saw her again a year later. I
 found out why she left me. It's a ████████ familiar story. She
 went with a guy with some money and got married. And went to
 his country.

-Where you angry when you met her again?

-No, I wasn't, when I saw her again, which was at Thermae about
 a year later, doing her job again...

-Even though she was married?

-Yeah, she told me he was back in America and ███████ didn't know.
 This happens a lot, apparently. She is giving him this story
 about - what was it- her mother was sick or something, and all
 she was, was out on the game.

-Was she simply bored in America?

-Yeah, bored, and now back on the game, every night, doing what
 she did before. We had a reunion for one night, she came back
 with me. I was with her this one night. She had changed, but I
 think I had changed even more. I didn't look at her the same way
 anymore. She wasn't the same person and I wasn't the same person.
 She seemed to be - maybe she always had been - totally materia-
 listic. And I was certainly more jaded about Thai women. I just
 couldn't trust... it was very difficult to trust her.

-But you still had sex with her? Weren't you hurt?

-I thought ████ maybe that might happen, but the following day
 when she left I thought, 'that's it'. I felt I would never see
 her again, never talk to her again. That was it, it didn't hurt
 me. It almost did the opposite, in fact.

-You saw through the illusion.

-That's right. I saw the illusion and I knew then, at that point,
 after that time that I would not be with her again, would not
 see her again.

-How did you wind up in prison?

-A prostitute turned me in to the police. I was arrested by the
 police in my apartment.

-Turned you in for what?

-I met this woman in Thermae and took her back to my apartment and something very strange happened. All of a sudden she got very panicky, started claiming I didn't have enough money. I told her: "I have money, I have money, no problem", but she didn't stay more than five minutes. She just walked out and I thought, well, she's not coming back. Five minutes later there was a knock on the door. I had been drinking, so I wasn't thinking very clearly. Without even looking I just opened the door. There she was with two Thai policemen. She probably just ran into them in the building. I had a little bit of ganja on the table, it wasn't much, but they spotted it. I hadn't any money to give them, so that was that. They took me to the police station. The first night I was there they demanded 35 000 Baht (about US$1400 at the time). I didn't have that much. I stayed in jail for seven days. Then they took me to court and the 35 000 went up to 50 000. At that point my boss was going to bail me out, but on the day of sentence they went from 50 000 to 100 000. He couldn't manage that much. It was a very, very terrible day. I thought I was gonna be getting out and I ended up handcuffed to a Dutch guy, put in a truck, and off to prison.

-How long were you sentenced for?

-That's one of the weirdest things about it, you're not really sure, no one tells you a thing. When I was put in prison, I heard different stories; I was going to be there a month, two months, a month and a half. I got all sorts of different answers on that. I didn't know until three weeks later how long it was going to be. I had no idea what was gonna happen. I started worrying about getting beaten up, raped, who knows? I didn't have a clue.

-So how was it in prison?

-At the time it was dreadful. Looking back maybe it wasn't as bad as I thought. But the biggest thing was the loss of freedom.

Losing freedom is maybe worse than anything in life. You know,
I have been poor, but losing freedom is just awful. The days go on
forever, it's so boring...

I had no problems with the Thai prisoners, they were nice to me.
But it was overcrowded and you see a lot of bad things, such as
how the Thai men are treated by the guards. I was there for a
month and a half, which is the minimum sentence for a small
amount of drugs. Most people I knew, Thais and falangs, were in
there for a lot longer, maybe they had heroin or something.

-But especially the falangs, how did they cope with their long
sentences?

-It's interesting; the ones who had been here for a while dealt
with it a lot better than those who had just come for a holiday.
They didn't have the patience, we told them: "you have to calm
down, the Thais are not gonna appreciate you yelling and getting
upset like this, you'll only make things worse." When I first
went in there, the first day, I was with this Dutch guy. He had
been in Thailand for a long time. We both talked about this and
agreed, no matter what happens, we stay as calm and polite as we
can. I think that really helped.

-What was he in for?

-He was arrested on Kaosarn Road in a guesthouse with twelve kilos.

-So, a long-term sentence?

-Here we go again, T.I.T., this is Thailand - he was released the
same time I was. He paid a fine of about 20 ooo Baht. They actually believed him when he said he was just giving this out to
his friends, wasn't interested in selling it, so he wasn't actually
charged with selling. He was lucky. And I think also, he was very
nice and polite to everyone, spoke good Thai. They look at this
and they make reports. When you go to court to speak to the judge,
you are very polite, don't say anything back, don't be sarcastic.
I think they notice that. In my case, after my sentence was up
and they took me back to the police station, at that point they

were going to deport me - that's what happens next, straight to immigration. And I can't believe it still, it's so bizarre, I was released by the commander of police out of the clear blue sky. They were taking me down to immigration, but they had made a mistake. They sent my passport to the US embassy. Immigration wouldn't accept me without it, they wouldn't take me, so I went back to the original jail. I was there about two days. Then on a Sunday, in the middle of the afternoon, they opened the cell. The commander spoke a little bit of English, said "you can go now." When he said that I thought I was heading back to X immigration. But no, He then said, in English, "You can go home now." I just couldn't believe it. They let m me out, onto the street.

-How long ago was that?

-Over three years ago.

-Have you renewed your D visa since then?

-No, the embassy still has my passport.

-But seriously, how do you think you can get your visa situation sorted out? To be able to get a job with an international school?

-Oh, sure, I can't get any job without doing that.

-But then, couldn't that mean that officially you are still in prison? Does the embassy know that you are out?

-Yes, they do. They were friendly. Of course they told me to straighten out my visa. Costs 20 ooo Baht as it does for anyone after a certain amount of time overstaying. But then they said, once I do that, I go out and come back in, no problems, don't worry about this small little charge. They are not going to care about such a small charge.

-In prison, you had contact with all the other foreigners. Were there cases where people couldn't cope with their sentences? How does a young guy handle a life sentence in a foreign country?

-I talked to a few who looked certain to be there for life. I was surprised how they seemed to handle it. They would compare this country to other south east Asian countries, think they're

better off here at least, than they would be in Cambodia, Vietnam or Indonesia. I think they took it that way. And then they
are also thinking, maybe somehow, they can get a lawyer to get
enough money together, get their sentences reduced. They even
hope that the ~~K~~ king will pardon them one of these years.

-So it's hope and illusion.

~~PAUSE~~

-A lot of hoping.

-Were there many beatings?

-I saw the guards beating Thai prisoners. I never saw anything
done to westerners. One of the reasons for that is that westerners have embassies here, and the Thais don't want the problem
of embassies finding out. If you are from the Middle East or
Africa, you might not have an embassy here, then there is a
chance that you might get beaten up or abused, because there is
nothing to fall back on.

-Did you see or hear of rapes?

-No, I never saw or heard of any. But I saw Thai men beaten up by
guards. Generally they came along and just hit them with their
batons.

-You once mentioned to me how you started understanding things
about Thai men and prostitution while in prison.

-We would sit in a rectangular room meant for 35 inmates, but it
was overcrowded so you had about fifty, very difficult to sleep.
You had no room at all. But at the same time you got to know,
got to talk to some of the Thai men. I remember two stories
particularly. One man had a decent job in Bangkok, in computers.
His wife was in the women's prison at the same time he was in
the men's. They had both been sitting on a bench at Sanam Luang
park. The police came over and planted heroin on them. They were
sent to prison. She was pregnant, which meant she'd have the baby
in prison. Actually I have heard of that more than once, drugs
being planted on these poor Thais. Then I heard this story of

another Thai man losing his woman, because she went off with a
falang. He was so hurt by that, he actually started to cry while
we were talking about it.

-Tell me this, how did you feel about your lifestyle at that moment?

-One of the things I learned in prison was a much better understanding of Thai men and what they must go through. For example
they would tell me about living up in their village, trying to
work to raise enough money for a dowry so they can marry the woman they love. Then not making enough and losing her because
somebody else comes along with more money.

-But you went to Thermae, you had been with all these women who
might have done the same thing to their husbands. How did you
feel about that?

-That's a good question. I didn't really think about that so much
at the time. I just thought that this was the first time I'd had
the chance to hear the other side of the story. All this time in
Thailand, only hearing the stories from the Thai women about
how bad Thai men were and what they did. Now for the first time
time I heard from Thai men about Thai women, the Thai men's
situation in this country, what they go through. How they were
just as much victims or even more so. And that was a real revela-
tion to me, I just hadn't had this opportunity before. I was
right there, as close as I could be, every day, every night. We
would joke a lot and talk about women, asking each other what we
thought about Thai women. It's funny, because a lot of the time
they would say the same things falang men would say, like: "Oh,
aren't they beautiful?" We just came over here, four or five
years, but they... is it possible they have grown up all their
lives being told the same things about Thai women?

-Another serious question, about AIDS. Did you always use condoms?

-No,I didn't. I changed when I first came here, when I first started carousing, going out a lot. No, I didn't use them. You

go out, you get too drunk, and you don't even bother.

-Did you ever get VD?

-I caught gonorrhoea twice. In the last few years I used condoms a
 lot more.

-Didn't it scare you, did you ever get tested?

-I was tested, but I haven't been back for a long time. I was tested, that was OK, but that was a long time ago. Funny, almost
 like a death wish. Why would you do that, knowing you might
 catch this disease? I really don't know. It's hard to answer this one, why I did that. I certainly did think about it and
 maybe, in a way, I thought I would be one of the lucky ones. Like
 Russian roulette. I'll be lucky, I won't get it. But who knows?

-What do you think about that now? Are you more scared?

-I probably am, I'm more conscious about it.

-Obviously you know that you might be infected now. How would you
 cope with having it? Would you be able to cope?

-I'm not sure how I would cope, but I have thought about it. If
 I did find out that I have it, I would probably go back to my
 home. Just because of the resources to take care of those kinds
 of things. I wouldn't stay here, I don't think I could trust the
 medical system.

-And what about the fact that you might have infected other women?

- That would be the worst thing. Not so much myself, but to think
 that you might have infected someone else. And of course, how do
 you know who, after a certain amount of time?

-Do you remember how many women you have slept with here in Thailand in the past five and a half years?

-I have slept with about IOO women, maybe 50% without condoms. It's
 interesting the attitude in that... there are girls who insist
 and that's good, and other girls who care less. And I even had
 girls with a real fatalistic attitude. One girl basically told me,
 I remember very well, "This is the way it's supposed to be, and
 if I'm supposed to die of AIDS I'll come back in another life

anyway, so this is my destiny."

-Your friends, other westerners in the nightlife, did they handle
 it in the same way or did they use condoms more often? Or did you
never speak about that issue?

-I remember one night, there were about five of us sitting around.
 We all asked that question to each other, and I think generally,
 it seems about half-and-half. There are some that are really conscious and do use them all the time, and there are others who
 hardly ever use them. I know a few who have never used them. Of
 course it's hard to know if they are honest or not about this. I
 am much better now, much better about using condoms. If I ever have
 a relationship with someone, with one person, and it got serious
 and I wanted to settle down, I would have to find out, I would
 have to know.

-Beforehand?

-Certainly. I think I would do that. I hope I would do that.

-How did you deal with that before you came to Thailand? In America
 did you use condoms? Were you AIDS-conscious there?

-No not really. I didn't really fuck around too much in America. I
 was with one girl for a long time and I never cheated on her. I
 was very loyal to her. And back in the 70's, before AIDS, I never
 used condoms. Nobody really thought of using them.

-How did you change? Before you were always steady with a girl and
 here you started sleeping around?

-I thought about that myself. I came over here, and it was as if I
 made a conscious decision to go a completely hedonistic way. I
 wasn't even here that long. The night after I arrived I was out
 shagging a prostitute. I didn't waste any time, I went straight
 for it. I wasn't frightened, I jumped right into it and didn't
 stop. I didn't even think of being afraid of disease. And I actually made a choice to just go for everything: utter bohemian
 hedonism.

-Looking back, do you think you made a mistake starting this kind of lifestyle in Thailand?

-If I turn out to have AIDS, that certainly would be true.

-But regarding your prison stay or falling in Love with the wrong girl?

-Yeah, you might want to step back a bit, think about what you're doing without going full speed ahead. Because at the end of the road there certainly will risk be involved, in every way. We've been talking about it. Your heart may be broken, getting into trouble with the police, sexual diseases. I guess part of that is, you can stay out all night, drink, and feel you can do what you want: the illusion of freedom. So you just keep going, you feel like there are no rules, you forget any rules you once kept to. You don't slow down, you just keep going. But sooner or later you are burned out, even if nothing terrible happens. You burn out eventually just because of the lifestyle. There has to be an end. Hopefully it's not a tragic end, you survive it. That's one of the reasons I had to leave Bangkok. There were some nights when I was out, even my friends were telling me near the end, the last few months in Bangkok I didn't know who I was, I was losing it. The drinking, I just had to get out. I'd been in Bangkok way too long. I will not necessarily give up on Thailand, but I just had to get out of that city, and the lifestyle I had adopted, which I'd been pursuing for five years without slowing down. And it was affecting my mind, it certainly affected my work. I wasn't working like I should have. But definitely more than anything it was affecting my mind, the stress was way too much. There seemed to be no end, going out at night seemed to be getting worse and worse in terms of drinking, relationships.

-Now in Pattaya you seem to have straightened out a bit. But if things here go wrong, is there a danger you may fall back into your old lifestyle?

-Yes there certainly is. I really have to be careful about that.

-Did you ever think about leaving Thailand?

-I thought about it. I'm probably still gonna stay here and see what happens as far as work is concerned. If I can get some kind of

serious job, like I said before, in an international school. I
am going to try for that. If I went back to my own country...
I'm older, and it's difficult to find work when you are over
forty years old. Also I don't have any family back home really.
Basically, if I go home, I will be on my own back there just as
I am here. And, practically speaking, the one thing that does
keep me here is that for me it's so cheap to stay compared to
the living expenses in America. The prospects of a job back in
America might not be that good.

-You don't have any family at all in America?

-I just have one sister, that's it.

-Do you have contact with her?

-We don't communicate that much. We're not that close. I mean,
 she thinks I'm absolutely insane, absolutely crazy. She doesn't
 understand it.

-She might be right about your being insane.

-Could be, yeah.

-To someone not in this lifestyle you're doing insane things.

-Well, I guess from her point of view that could be true, although
 her lifestyle, where she is living, I think is insane. Where she
 lives in the suburbs, this very normal routine lifestyle, which
 most people have, I've never liked that. I can't adapt to it,
 and I think that would just make me crazy, I have always enjoyed
 the bohemian lifestyle.

-Do you have an alcohol problem in Thailand?

-Oh yes, definitely. I have always drunk alcohol, since I was six-
 teen, but the amount has increased a lot since I have been here.
 I suppose in America I was still drinking a lot in terms of, ﬞ
 let's say weekends filled out with drink, but here, because of the
 lifestyle, and everything is open 24 hours a day, any day of the
 week, it's easy to fall into it. You like alcohol, you can drink
 anytime you want. And not just myself, I know so many people,
 and everyone says the same thing. They are drinking a lot more

than they used to.

-Cutting back to an old question, do you think if you had stuck
with your original plan, travelling around Asia, that your life
would have turned out better or happier?

-It's hard to say. I don't know. Because I don't necessarily
regret the stay here. I had some really wonderful experiences.
It hasn't all been negative. One of the good things about being
in prison was the people I met. I would say I am still happy
that I came here. At times I have thought about leaving, going
to another Asian country, but I am still here. And as of now,
I have no plans to leave soon. Of course this is a change for
me and I will see what happens here in Pattaya. Hopefully I will
be a bit more organised.

-Do you see your life up to now as a failure?

-There certainly have been failures, a lot of lows, and there have
been a few highs. Generally speaking, there's a lot of lows. But
the worst problem, as you get older, is not so much failure or
success in terms of jobs, money and so on. I think the worst
problem is loneliness. That's what you have to deal with. I

have never been married, never had family. You have to deal with
loneliness, the most difficult thing.

-Does that fact also keep you here in Thailand, that you're scared of being lonely in America?

-Good point. I did feel lonelier in America than I have been
here. ~~████████ █████ ██████, ████████ ████ █████ █████ █████ █████ █████████~~
~~████████~~

-If you went back, would you fall into much deeper solitude?

-Yes, and I'm also not sure that I could even cope with ~~██████~~
living back there. I'm getting so used to living here. That loneliness I experienced before could be a lot worse going back,
because it has been such a long time. And the people I used to
be with back in America, they have gone their separate ways.
I could end up in a big city looking for work and not knowing
anyone. I wouldn't like that at all.

-Are you scared?

-Yeah, I am in a way.

-By coming here, did you bring yourself into a hopeless situation, a situation you can't turn back anymore?

-I wouldn't want to go back so much now. At first I was thinking of going back, and after a couple of years being here, I'm not sure if I could cope with going back. I think it would be far worse being poor and without work in America than to be here. If nothing else I could somehow manage to get some money here even if it's just teaching English. You get a little bit, you can still live cheaply.

-So you balance it?

-Yes, that's right. It's a practical matter, that's what I keep telling myself. Balance is what you gotta try and achieve, not going overboard with the drinking and going out at night too much. If you can manage that you'll be OK.

-The last five years you couldn't manage that?

-Yeah, that's right. We'll see what happens here. I noticed the change here myself, I still believe Bangkok had a lot to do with it. I may be wrong, but I think that it almost killed me. I had to get out.

EARRING ANDY, SUKHUMUIT 7/11/99
THE FIRST NIGHT OUT AFTER HE LEFT HIS
WIFE AND CHILDREN

"I HAVE NOT BEEN WITH A WOMAN FOR NINE MONTHS."

"I DON'T KNOW WHAT MADE ME CHANGE HERE. BEFOR I WOULD HAVE NEVER TOUCHED A WOMAN WITHOUT CONDOMS, HERE I HAVE NEVER USED THEM."

"I AM HERE BECAUSE I FUCKED UP, LITERALLY."

"NEXT MONTH MY BROTHER COMES TO VISIT ME, TO PERSUADE ME TO LEAVE BANGKOK. I HAVEN'T SEEN A MEMBER OF MY FAMILY FOR 4 YEARS. MY MOTHER WANTS ME TO RE-TURN HOME. MY DAD NEEDS SOMEONE TO TAKE OVER HIS BUSINESS. BUT HOW CAN I LIVE BACK HOME AFTER ALL THESE EXPERIEN-CES?"

"I HAVE BEEN OUT OF THE COMPUTER BUSINESS FOR TOO LONG, EVERY SCHOOL BOY KNOWS MORE THAN ME."

"FOR ME IT'S ENGLISH TEACHING OR NOTHING."

"I HAVE NOTHING, ONLY BABY IN STOMACH. I WALK, WALK. I SIT, SOMEBODY GIVE ME BEER, SOME MONEY. I STAY HERE FOREVER. MAYBE I DIE SOON. I'M NEARLY 25 YEARS NOW. SINCE 15 YEARS I STAY IN BANGKOK. MAKE A GO-GO, SELL BODY. I ONLY SMOKE JAA MAA, NO HEROIN, COCAINE. I'M SICK IN MY STOMACH, IN HERE, I DON'T KNOW HOW TO SAY. I DIE SOON. YESTERDAY POLICE CATCH ME, BUT LET ME GO, GIVE ME MO. NEY FOR FOOD."

AEH, 10/3/99

13/3/93, AEH IN KING'S LOUNGE (THE HAPPIEST GIRL IN TOWN)

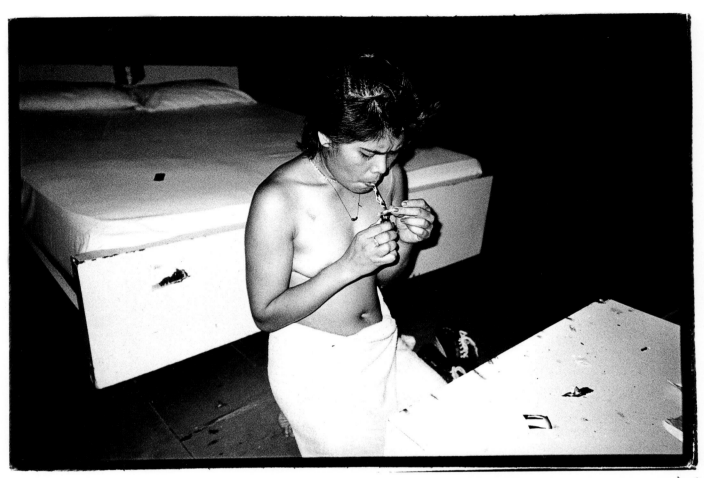

AEH, SMOKING AMPHETAMINES, MALAYSIA HOTEL AREA, 10/3/99

The last I heard of George is that he lives
on a beach in Mexico.

Robert was deported to America. I never
heard of him again.

Earring Andy is still around.

Bruce went back to Australia, after being
beaten to a pulp by tuk-tuk drivers. He
went back to university to do a degree in
Thai studies, and wants to come back.

Scott is still in Pattaya, has a girlfriend
and will soon become a father. His AIDS test
turned out negative.

Many older girls have disappeared, but fresh
ones are constantly arriving from the
villages of the north and north-east.

Thank you so much:

Carlos Mustienes,
who brought my dream to reality

Bert Heinzlmaier,
for opening my eyes

Oli Pin Fat,
always helping me out, pushing
me in the right direction

My dad,
constantly saving *me* from ruin

Nit,
for having sorted out my life,
and still putting up with me.
I love you

(THE VISION!)
Gigi, Mark, Nick, Amanda

And all the people who so ~~kindly~~
kindly permitted me to be a part
of their lives, to photograph
them, who believed in me and my
work

I could not have done this book without you

WE FUCKED UP,

LIFE FUCKED US,

SO WE FUCKED LIFE !

First published in Great Britain in 2000 by
Westzone Publishing Ltd
I9 Clifford Street, London WIX IRH, UK

© Nick Nostitz

IO 9 8 7 6 5 4 3 2 I

A catalogue record for this book is available
from the British Library

ISBN 0 9537438 2 9

Cover design by
Rose Design, London

Colour separations by
Fotolito Express, Padova

Printed in Italy by
L.E.G.O., Vicenza